When the perishable has been clothed
with the imperishable, and the mortal
with immortality, then the saying that
is written will come true: "Death has
been swallowed up in victory".

(1 Co 15, 54)

The Resurrection

or the immortality of the body

Gilles Charles Vuille

THE RESURRECTION

or

the immortality of the body

From the same author:

THE RESURRECTION
OR
THE IMMORTALITY
OF THE BODY

Gilles Charles Vuille

ISBN: 978-1-959483-93-9 (sc)

Library of Congress Control Number: 0000000000

Contents

Introduction 1

Death ... and then? 5

Purgatory 17

Hell 25

Heaven 33

Resurrection 41

Immortality 49

Introduction

Resurrection, immortality, both sensitive topics - as one can imagine - but which remain nonetheless the foundation if not the backbone of the Christian religion, as taught by Jesus Christ through his disciples. A large extract of this can be found in St Paul'Epistles, 1 Corinthians, 15. Further to Emperor Constantin's decree set up in 320 A.D., recognizing Christianity "the Empire's official religion", the dogma of the Faith had to be established. At the first Council of Nicaea in 325 A.D. the religious officials of yesteryear drafted the famous Nicene Creed; the Apostles' Creed followed in the 9th Century:

I believe in God the Father Almighty, Creator of Heaven and earth; I believe in Jesus Christ, His only Son, our Lord, He was conceived by the power of the Holy Spirit and born of the Virgin Mary. He suffered under Pontius Pilate, was crucified, died, and was buried. He descended to the dead. On the third day He rose again. He ascended into Heaven and is seated at the right hand of the Father. He will come again to judge the living and the dead. I believe in the Holy Spirit, the Holy Catholic Church, the communion of Saints, the forgiveness of sins, the resurrection of the body, and the life everlasting. Amen.

It should be noted that at the end the Nicene Creed contains this specificity which is not insignificant:

I believe to the Church, One, Holy, catholic, and apostolic.

Thus, in a few words, everything is said, resurrection and eternal life included. Therefore, how can it be that so many people are afraid of death, when Jesus Christ offers immortality to anybody willing to follow his precepts?

Centuries have passed and Councils have followed. Theology (the study of God) goes on. Teachings have been and are still being given, while seminars, conferences, and symposiums are being held. Books, hundreds or even thousands, have been written on this subject. Although the teaching of Christian religion is given to everyone, and even more so to those with a calling, it must be noted that subjects such as resurrection and immortality do not interest anybody anymore, just like death – an intrinsically linked subject, still taboo – which does not occupy the central role it ought to.

Since the seventies or the eighties religious teaching (like other disciplines, morality included) has also declined, and the above mentioned subject – because of its difficulty – seems to no longer be of interest to neither religious officials nor to believers, following indeed our lifestyle, resolutely modern, more stupid than wise, where everything fades, North turning into South, and East into West. It is therefore quite necessary to set the record straight and to condense what we know about the said subject into a summary for a better understanding of its ins and outs.

The Resurrection – in the Christian meaning of the word – is coming back to life after death. Before resurrecting - because all of us will have to resurrect in order to be judged according to what we had done (Ap 20, 12-13) and nothing else – the human being (from what is known today, just like yesterday) has to die and we cannot deal with a subject like death as we would with our next vacation. As previously stated, death remains a taboo subject which is upsetting. Yes, for many of us it first upsets our conscience. Fortunately, the traditional teachings are still in force, whether the usual suspects like it or not, you can be sure of it!

This booklet will therefore mention the steps for Human Being, that leads from death to the Resurrection, then even to the eternal life.

Furthermore, let us add to this introduction this text from the Swiss writer Georges Haldas. From his book: *Socrates and the Christ*[1]:

(...) Socrates has consecrated his life to the search of the truth, while Christ came to this world to witness the truth (...) For each of them, our terrestrial life – short-life – is only a preparation to another life, which is still waiting for us beyond the death.

---

[1] Editions L'Age d'Homme, Lausanne, Switzerland, 2002.

This preparation to another life is what is taught by Christianity to its believers, among other things. If everything or nearly everything has been said already about the soul, one must now accept as true what has been said and what will follow, otherwise the following account becomes infertile and therefore cannot become fruitful, thus is the same spirit as St Paul said to the Corinthians, namely :

But if there be no resurrection of the dead, then is Christ not risen: And if Christ be not risen, then is our preaching vain, and your faith is also vain (1 Co 15, 13-14).

* * *

Death ... and then?

So, our ancestors the Greeks already had some idea about the soul; it was (and still is) part of the physical body, having itself "a body". When the physical death occurs, the soul – as immortal – returns to the Creator[2], with a first judgment, then – for a few – a first resurrection[3] (for example the saints), to finally enter *in my Father's house [where] are many mansions*, said Christ[4].

Ezra, an Hebrew scribe and a man of the Bible, one of the prophets of his time and in fact an expert of the Moses' Law, had, upon returning from the Babylonian Captivity, ca 538 BC, date of the Decree of Cyrus, which allowed the Hebrew to return to Jerusalem, carried bitter reproach towards God. Obviously, death frightened him too. Here is his remarkable dialogue[5]:

---

[2] Lc 12, 20. *But God said unto him, Thou fool, this night thy soul shall be required of thee: then whose shall those things be, which thou hast provided?*

[3] Ap 20, 6.

[4] Jn 14, 2.

[5] IV Esdras, 7, 75-139, Ecrits inter testamentaires, (Intertestamental Scriptures), La Pléiade, Editions Gallimard, Paris, 1987, p. 1425-31.

If I have found grace before you, Lord, still show this to your servant; after death—when each of us returns his soul—shall we be kept in rest until comes that time in which you will begin to renew creation, or shall we immediately be tormented? He answered me: I shall still reveal it to you: but do not confuse yourself with those who despised commands and do not count yourself among those who will be tormented. [As we can see we already have here those who have done well—the small remnant—and those who have done bad – the stubborn people]. Because the treasure of your works rests with the Almighty, but it will not be shown to you before the last days.

About death, here is the teaching: when the decisive judgment is pronounced by the Almighty so that a man dies; when the soul leaves the body and returns to the one who had given it at first to adore the Most High; If the man was of those who disdained the ways of the Most High and did not follow them, of those who despised his law and who hated those who are afraid of God, then these souls do not enter into my habitations but, suffering and sad, they roam immediately in agonies of seven sorts (...) As for the souls of those who followed the ways of the Most High, this is what is ordered for the time when they must be separated from the corruptible flesh. While they lived there, they toiled to serve the Most High, facing danger at all times to keep perfectly the law of the Legislator. That is why, such is the teaching concerning them: they see at first, with great joy, the glory of the One who receives them and they rest in seven ways.

Finally, as Ezra is a very curious man and continues asking subtle questions, another dialogue follows:

The Judge, finally, because if he did not forgive those who were created by his word and if he did not erase their uncountable injustices, maybe among the infinite multitude, would there remain only a few people? The angel answered me:

The Almighty made the present world for many people, but the future world for a few of them. I will tell you a parable, Ezra: If you question the earth it will answer you that it produces in great quantities the clay from which we make pottery, but in a small quantity the dust from which gold is drawn. Such is also the rule of the present world: many are created, but few are saved.

Between the beautifully thought and formulated questions at the time and the given answers, to be clear, it is clear! At least for now ...

As it is also matter of "home" here are what the Blessed Jan van Ruysbroeck[6] (1293-1387) already had to say about it:

When God created the soul out of nothing, and united with the body, He set a determined day and a certain hour for it, and these are only known to Him, and then the soul must relinquish time, and reveal itself in His presence. The opportunity of the case is required

---

[6] *The Spiritual Espousals*, Faber and Faber Ltd, London, 1952.

because the soul must speak and answer for the words and all the works that ever it performed, in the presence of the eternal verity.

As it was subjects, in previous texts, of seven types of torments and seven types of resting souls, let us now see another explanation given by the Blessed Jan van Ruysbroeck for the five categories of people subject to judgment:

The first class, and the worst, are those Christian men who die in mortal sin without contrition and without repentance, because they have despised the death of Christ and His sacraments or have received them vainly and without proper disposition. And they have not shown works of mercy in charity to their fellow-Christians according to God's ordinance, and therefore they are condemned to the nethermost pit in hell.

The next class are those without the Faith, heathens or heretics. They must all appear before Christ. Yet they were condemned all the days of their lives, for they had neither grace nor Divine love: therefore dwelt always in the everlasting death of damnation. But they shall be less tormented than evil Christians, because they had received fewer gifts from God and be less of what they owed to God.

The third class are good Christians who sometimes have fallen into sin, and have risen up again with contrition and acts of penance, and have not fulfilled their penance as justice required. Their place is in purgatory.

The fourth class are those who have kept God' commandments or, even if they have broken them, have turned again to God with contrition and with penitence and with works of charity and mercy, and have completed their penance, so that their souls, issuing forth, go straight to heaven without any purgation.

The fifth class are those who have their conversation in heaven, above all outward works of charity, and are united and sunk in God, and God in them, so that between God and them time and our mortal state can interpose no means. When such are released from their bodies, in the same moment they enjoy their eternal blessedness. And they are not judged, but on the last day they shall with Christ give judgment upon other men.

This is a rather "gentle" vision since it only deals with categories of "judged men" and this deserves some additional information, as we will see from the following texts.

After this 14th Century vision, let us now take a look at one from this century, from a new "messenger", the French-Canadian Francine Bériault who will give us another view on the subject, taken from her book, "Love for All My Children, Jesus"[7] describing with more details events to come.

Whether we know it or not, whether we perceived it already or not, it appears that soon, very soon, men

---

[7] Editions FJ, Sherbrooke, Québec, Canada, 2004, p. 52ss.

will have to answer to God for their actions during their earthly life. Moreover, for many years now, mankind has been called to Reconciliation as well as to Conversion. These new prophets have also told us that significant events were upon us, in full accordance with biblical texts[8]. In fact, this will come as a Warning, as it is important for us to understand that we will all experience the enlightenment of our consciences at the same time. Later will come the Great Purification of the flesh. This is exactly what is described by Francine Beriault in the fourth volume of her above-mentioned book, which was dictated by Christ, still alive of course, as He resurrected from the dead. Let us take a look!

- *I declare to you; I, the God of strength, the God of light, I will make my almightiness descend upon each of you and my light will permeate you. Like a bolt of lightning, you will all enter within yourselves; you will be in a great light and the God of Love will reveal himself to you. Your lives will start to unfold before your eyes; it will be like high tide, you will not be able to stop any of it. All will be before you and, at the same time, you will be taking part in it. All that you have done which is not love, from your birth until that day, will have to be eradicated from you; if you pronounce your 'yes', then you shall live eternally. Not a single one of you is unknown to me, I know*

---

[8] Ac 2,17-18 And it shall come to pass in the last days, saith God, I will pour out of my Spirit upon all flesh: and your sons and your daughters shall prophesy, and your young men shall see visions, and your old men shall have dreams:

who bears a yes or a no; but, as I am a just God, I want you to be free to pronounce it. I, the Power, will place within that light a power that will help you to know your answer; yes, each one of you will know his answer with clarity.

- All those who will have pronounced a burning yes, I will permeate them with such a light of peace and love that they will come to know happiness at that very moment. The light will shine forth from them, there will be nothing but wonder. Because they will have already pronounced their yes and they will also have accepted to live their purification, God will reveal to them all they endured out of love. They will see to what extent God encompassed them with his love throughout their purification. What joy they will feel in the face of all God has done for them since their birth, and how grateful they will be to have accepted the love of God. Because they have given themselves, The Love will give himself to them, and they will receive him so that in turn, they may give themselves more fully: the apotheosis of love!

- All those who will have pronounced a hesitant yes, without seeking to know if they were truly sincere, these will see the light joyfully. They will be struck by the light and everything will begin within them. They will see themselves as children lacking love and they will regret, with so much love, having offended God that they will feel the joy of repentance. They will experience a moment of deep purification, for these children will experience joy and, at the same time, the sorrows of love. This joy will be within them, and, because they will see what they have done against The Love and what they have not done for The Love, these sorrows of love will equally be within them. They will give themselves to The Love and The Love will take them to never, no never let them go.

- All those who will have carried a yes within them but, due to a lack of courage, will not have pronounced it, will have a light within them that will remind them that they are God's children; they who will have wanted to ignore him will not be able to ignore themselves before The Love. God will cover them with his love to show them that he loves them and that he himself nourished their yes, for God was aware of their lack of courage over pronouncing their yes, these will discover God's love for them with a burning wound in their hearts. Their purification will be according to the measure of their works of love for their neighbour and for God but, because they ignored themselves by not wanting to pronounce their yes, they will suffer. Their sufferings will be accompanied by graces of love, they will be joyful to discover that they are children of love filled with inner courage, and this courage will never leave them.

- All those who will not have wanted to pronounce their yes because of a lack of proof of God's coming within them, these will experience heartbreak over not having taken their yes seriously; they will see *all God wanted to give them and all they could have discovered if they had not lacked faith. They will have sufferings, but their sufferings will be necessary to them in order to become, once again, children of faith in the power of God; they will discover God's unconditional love. They will be at peace before of all they will see, for they will feel God's protection; they will even want to offer their sorrows without knowing their reward. God will show them what they have earned because of this loving gesture; an indefinable peace will cover them and they will never again have the need for proof of God's love for them.*

- *All those who will have said a hypocritical yes, while they were nourishing a no, I, the God of Power, I will make them see all their shortcomings towards The Love. Because they will have wanted to show devotion to God and to their neighbour while they harboured nothing but a distaste for God's love, due to this hypocritical rejection of The Love, they will discover all they could have had: happiness, joy, peace, love and eternal life. An enormous sadness will permeate them, it will be so great that their bodies will be afflicted with pain so atrocious that they will want to disappear; but none of these children will escape, for The Love will have seized them. As they will have said no to The Love, they will not be able to penetrate the New Earth.*

- *All those who will not have a yes within them, but rather a no, they, the ones who are indifferent to*

The Love, they will suffer greatly. Because of their indifference towards God's love, towards the love of one's neighbour and towards love for themselves, nothing within them will show them a profound desire to become love, for God knows them. Their indifference towards all that is of God will have made them cold; they will remain stony before God's love for them and before his Presence. As they will want nothing to do with the fire of love, they will feel sufferings that will be what they are: pure ice. These sufferings will bring about no sense of regret within them, they will have nothing but hatred against The Love, who will make them discover what they are. Oh! These children should never have known life, nothingness would have been a better place for them than the place in which they will be for eternity.

• *All those who will not have a yes within them, but rather a voluntary no, will come to know the depth of their refusal. They who nourished their no joyfully, refusing the sacraments, ridiculing my Church and their neighbour, waging war against those who were weaker than they, these children will be God's outlaws, for they have fought my children; they have renounced my laws going as far as destroying me in their lives: they will come to know my wrath. The Love will show them that their presence is unworthy of him, which will make them very unhappy. All their misdeeds will be like bites on their flesh to them and their sufferings will render them inert, for God will not want to hear their hatred against him; because of this, they will feel pain like a rod that will whip them; they will inflict this upon themselves and they will know this. These children will have nothing but sorrows as nourishment for ever and ever.*

- *All those who will have openly uttered a hateful no to The Love by making vile gestures to the true Presence and by offering to the Devil their soul, because they have offended the holy Body of Christ, because they have sacrificed their soul while it belonged to God, they, the vile traitors, the renegades, will experience such great sufferings that they will call out to death to come to their aid, but death will laugh at them, for it will be preparing itself to inflict upon them what they have done to God, in order that they may be severely punished, for death is God's wrath for those who reject him. It would have been better if they had never been born. Their sorrows will be indefinable. The most atrocious sorrow will be to endure God's gaze upon them, God will shine with love for them; they will come to know the love that will extinguish itself and their souls will feel this. Oh! How horrible it will be for them!*

From Ruysbroeck's "gentle" account to Francine Bériault's one, it is not at all the same matter. It has become serious, even grave. We often reproach the Church and its officials and sometimes even God, to be old fashioned and out of touch. Here, with this new approach (God never stops to manifest Himself all along our journey, we have forgotten it!), God – who always provides – comes to warn us of what we are about to face. In this respect, we should note that even our ancestors – the Hebrew – were troubled with it, as one of them (David) had this question[9].

What is man, that thou art mindful of him? and the son of man, that thou visitest him?

Those who have ears should hear! Or, in other words, those who need to understand, understand! Thus, as read in terms of "purification" this will occur before being admitted to the Kingdom of God, which seems obvious, the soul must be clean, pure in God's eyes. To that end, it is indeed in Purgatory that this should take place.

* * *

---

[9] Ps 8,5 – He 2,5.

Purgatory

Traditional definition: A *place where souls completely atone for their sins.*

Some say that the purgatory is not mentioned within the Bible. That is fine! Must God really write down everything, say everything, so that people understand? Among us all, who knows God's designs?

The Catechism booklet of the Catholic Church reveals the following:

The Church calls this final purification of the elect "Purgatory" which is quite distinct from the punishment of the damned. The Church formulated the doctrine of the Faith relating to Purgatory, especially at the Councils of Florence (1439) and Trent (1545). The tradition of the Church, referring to certain texts from the Scriptures (1 Cor 3, 15 - 1 P 1,7), speaks of a purifying fire[10].

Wise men and prophets from the O.T. through whom God revealed Himself – in full accordance with the

---

[10] Editions Centurion/Cerf, Paris, 1998, # 1031, p. 262.

Scriptures (Amos 3,7)[11] - let us first think about these words credited to Salomon, King David's son.

After slight corrections, they [the elect of God] will receive great benefits. God tested them and found them worthy of him; like crucible gold, he purified them (Sg 3, 5-6).

Next let us see Ezekiel's words (Ez 36, 25) :

Then will I sprinkle clean water upon you, and ye shall be clean: from all your filthiness, and from all your idols, will I cleanse you.

As well as these ones: (Ez 37, 23) :

They shall not defile themselves anymore with their idols and their detestable things, or with any of their transgressions. But I will save them from all the backslidings in which they have sinned, and will cleanse them; and they shall be my people,

Even Daniel mentioned it (Dn 11, 35) :

And some of them of understanding shall fall, to try them, and to purge, and to make them white, even to the time of the end: because it is yet for a time appointed.

---

[11] *Surely the Lord God will do nothing, but he revealeth his secret unto his servants the prophets.*

The prophets of the N.T. through whom God revealed Himself, even nowadays, are also in full accordance with the Scriptures, as already noted on page 10 (Acts 2, 17-18)[12]. To continue this topic of the Purgatory, and to validate what has just been exposed, here are other revelations from people "chosen" by Heaven.

Let us start with the Italian mystic Sainte Catherine of Genoa (1447-1510)[13] :

The necessity of purgatory: Here I add what I see. On God's side, paradise is open; anyone who wishes may enter. Because God is mercy He is turned towards us with open arms to welcome us into His glory. But I see on the other hand how this divine Spirit is of such a purity and clarity, beyond anything we could imagine, that a soul which had in itself an imperfection as slight as a minuscule fleck of straw would leap into a thousand hells rather than face this divine majesty with such a flaw. Therefore, seeing that purgatory was created to take away such flaws, the soul leaps in. It understands that here is a great mercy for it to be rid of such a hindrance...

---

[12] *And it shall come to pass in the last days, saith God, I will pour out of my Spirit upon all flesh: and your sons and your daughters shall prophesy, and your young men shall see visions, and your old men shall have dreams:*

[13] *Sainte Catherine of Genoa*, Editions Descléede Brouwer, Paris, 1960, p. 208.

Now, in order to get an additional explanation, let us read – in the book "Portrait of Marthe Robin", Ed. Grasset & Fasquelle, Paris, 1985, p. 81 -- what this French mystic (1902-1981) saw within that place:

I am not eager to experience Purgatory, and yet I will have to face it. I do not like the word 'purgatory'; it makes me remember the purges I was given when I was little; but purgatory is not a purge. It is something far different, huge, serious, I would even say noble. There is pain, but they are pains of love, of true love, pure love. Souls want to reach God; they jostle one another but cannot manage it. If you could only see their downfall! They are sent back; it is not yet the time. The more that come out, the more enter. We should rather say "purificatory". Everything must be purified. Even our intentions should be purified. We do not know if our intentions have really been totally pure (...) I told you that I do not want to avoid Purgatory.

To establish – once and for all – this subject as well as this place on which mere speculations and incredible statements have been made, here is what Christ dictated to another Italian mystic Maria Valtorta[14] (1890-1962), in 1943:

The souls immersed in those flames suffer only from love. Not undeserving of possessing the Light, but not entirely worthy to enter immediately into the Kingdom

---

[14] *The Notebooks 1943*, Maria Valtorta, CEV, Isola del Liri, Italy, 2002, p. 394 and next.

of Light, these souls, on presenting themselves to God, are assailed by the Light. This is a brief, advance blessedness which makes them certain of their salvation, makes them aware of what their eternity will be like and knowledgeable regarding what they did to their souls, defrauding them of years of blessed possession of God. Then, immersed in the place of purgation, they are assailed by the flames of expiation. (...) They are a fire of Love. (...) It is through loving in Purgatory that you may conquer the Heaven, which in life you were unable to merit (...).

This gives us a clear enough look of the place, without doubt or ambiguity.

Finally, let me bring a beautiful soul to your attention, Maria Simma (1915–2004), an Austrian woman relatively unknown to the general public, but known worldwide for her relationship with souls in purgatory. She was blessed with an exceptional gift, the ability to converse with souls in this intermediary place. Here some of her visions[15]:

A few important things that the holy souls have taught her over the years:

The holy souls have repeatedly told her that the greatest help for them that they can obtain from those here on

---

[15] Les âmes du Purgatoire m'ont dit, (The souls of Purgatory told me), Editions Christiana, Stein am Rein, Suisse (Switzerland), 1998, p. 52.

earth is the offering of holy Mass. Next to the Mass, the holy Rosary and the Stations of the Cross are very beneficial to them. Any sacrifice we make—even the smallest ones offered—specifically for them have a great value in the eyes of God, and greatly lessen their sufferings and time in purgatory. The poor souls have told her that even the smallest prayer or sacrifice is like giving a cool glass of water to a parched sojourner travelling in the driest desert.

The greatest grievance from souls in purgatory: abandonments by their loved one.

The poor souls have told Maria that because they no longer possess a physical body, they can no longer make sacrifices for themselves in reparation for their sins; nor can they physically give an offering in request for a holy Mass; for themselves essentially they are able only to offer up to God their prayers and the repentance for their sins, so in many ways they are almost helpless, and are forced to rely on the mercy of God, the most extraordinary and blessed help of the Virgin Mary, the prayers of the Saints in heaven, and the prayers and sacrifices of the Church and of all the peoples here upon the earth.

According to Maria, the holy souls have revealed to her the following:

That priests and nuns should always wear their habits/clerics in as much as possible.

That Extraordinary Eucharistic Ministers should be used very rarely, that is, only when it is absolutely necessary; that priests and deacons should make every effort to distribute Communion to the faithful, even though it takes longer to do so.

That receiving Holy Communion in the hand should be avoided as much as possible.

That holding hands during the Lord's prayer and that the sign of peace after the Eucharistic prayer should be avoided in as much as it is possible, since both of these are a distraction from Jesus who is present upon the altar and that we should be concentrating upon Jesus alone during this important time of the Mass.

That outside of the Blessed Virgin Mary, Saint Joseph is one of the greatest Saints who advocates for the souls in Purgatory.

The Angels, especially St Michael the archangel, and also the poor souls own guardian angel are also very powerful in helping to obtain mercy and pleading their cause before God. Also very important is any Saint that the person might have had a devotion to during one's lifetime. Maria also pointed out that the Patron Saint of the poor souls in purgatory is St Nicholas of Tolentino.

The holy souls have also revealed to Maria that it is on Christmas day that the most souls are released from purgatory and then also Good Friday, Ascension day, All Souls day and the feast of the Assumption.

After this description of Purgatory, now to the less pleasant place, respectively the most horrific and certainly the more famous: hell.

*   *   *

Hell

This one, everybody knows it, at least by name. Indeed, everybody speaks about it, as biblical texts also mentioned it. Here too, let us first read its "human" definition!

Hell is, according to many religions, a state of extreme suffering of the human spirit after its separation from the body, pain experienced after death by those who have committed crimes and sins in their earthly life.

Again, to get the best possible explanation, it is still Christ – never sparing with His teachings – who will talk about it. Dictated to Maria Valtorta in January 1944[16]:

The men of this time no longer believe in the existence of Hell. They have invented an afterlife according to their taste, such as to be less terrifying for their conscience, which deserves much punishment. (...) they know that their conscience would draw back from certain misdeeds if it really believed in Hell in the way that Faith teaches (...) I have said that the fire is eternal and that all the scandalmongers and workers of iniquity shall find themselves there. I have told you that purgatory is a fire

---

[16] The Notebooks 1944, CEV, Isola del Liri, Italy, 2003, p. 76.

of love. But hell is a fire of severity. (...) Hell is a place where the thought of God is remorse, anger, damnation, and hatred. Hatred for Satan, hatred of mankind and hatred of oneself. (...) Even I, who created that place, tell you that when I descended into it to bring out of Limbo those who awaited my coming, I, God, experienced horror at that horror; and if something made by God were not immutable, on account of being perfect, I would have wanted to make it less atrociounnes, for I am Love, and I was pained by that horror.

This could not be clearer! Now let us read what the Blessed Anne Catherine Emmerich (1774-1824), a little countrywoman from Westphalia, Germany, but also one of the greatest mystics of the catholic world, left us regarding this terrifying place[17].

I saw that among the demons chained by Christ, during his descent into hell, some were untied not long ago and aroused this sect. I saw that others will be released from two generations to two generations (October 19, 1823).

She saw, with their terrible consequences, the measures which the propagators of the lights took, wherever they came to power and influence, to abolish the divine worship as well as all the practices and the exercises of piety, or to make it something as vain as were the big words of "light", "charity", "spirit", under which they sought to hide from themselves and from others the

---

[17] *Catherine Emmerich's prophecies for our time,* Raoul Auclair, Nouvelles Editions Latines, Paris, 1974, p. 56 and next.

desolate emptiness of their businesses or God was for nothing .

My guide led me around the whole earth: I had to ceaselessly go through immense caves made of darkness and where I saw an immense quantity of people wandering on all sides and occupied with dark works. It seemed like I was traveling all over the inhabited points of the globe, seeing nothing but the world of vice.

Often I saw new troops of men fall from above into this blindness of vice. I did not see that nothing was improving ... I had to go into darkness and once again consider malice, blindness, perversity, set traps, vindictive passions, pride, deceit, envy, greed, discord, murder, lust and horrible impiety of men, all things which however were of no benefit to them, but made them more and more blind and miserable and plunged them into darkness deeper and deeper. Often I had the impression that entire cities were placed on a very thin crust of earth and ran the risk of soon collapsing in the abyss.

I saw these men dig themselves slightly covered pits for others: but I did not see any good people in this darkness, nor any, therefore fall into the pits. I saw all these wicked people like big dark spaces stretching from side to side; I saw them pell-mell as in the tumultuous confusion of a great fair, forming various groups which were excited with the evil and masses which mixed one with the other; they committed all kinds of guilty acts and each sin resulted in another. Often it seemed to me that I was sinking even deeper into the night. The path went down a steep slope; it was something horribly scary and spread around the whole world. I live with people of all colors, wearing the most diverse costumes and all immersed in these abominations.

Often I would wake up full of anguish and terror; I saw the moon shining peacefully through the window, and I prayed to God, groaning not to let me see these frightening images again. But soon I had to go back down to these terrible dark spaces and see the abominations that were committed there. I once found myself in such a horrible sphere of sin that I thought I was in hell and started to cry and moan.

It seemed to me that I saw a very large place that received more daylight. It was like the image of a city belonging to the part of the world we live in. A horrible spectacle was shown to me there. I saw our Lord Jesus Christ crucified. I shivered to the marrow: because there were only men of our time there. He was a martyrdom of the Lord much more dreadful and much more cruel than the one he had to suffer in Jerusalem.

I live there with horror a great number of people I know, even priests. Lots of lines and ramifications from people who wandered in darkness ended up there.

I saw an innumerable crowd of unfortunate oppressed, tormented and persecuted today in several places, and I always saw by that how they abused Jesus Christ in person. We are in a deplorable time when there is no longer a refuge from evil: a thick cloud of sin hangs *over the whole world, and I see men doing the most abominable things with complete tranquility and indifference.*

I live all this in several visions while my soul was led through various countries all over the world.

I live new martyrs, not in the present time (1820, the year when Anne-Catherine had this vision) but in the time to come. However, I see that they are already oppressed.

And a last example: *Treaty of Hell*[18], by the Italian mystic Françoise Romaine (1384-1440). Here is a short extract:

One day when the servant of God was very suffering, she locked herself in her cell, to give herself up freely to the exercise of contemplation, where she found her consolation and all her delights. It was about four o'clock in the afternoon: she was immediately delighted in ecstasy, and the archangel Raphael, whom she did not see then, came to take her and led her to the vision of hell. Arriving at the door of this dreadful kingdom, she read these words written in fiery characters: "This place is hell, where there is no rest, no consolation, no hope". This door being open, she looked and saw an abyss so deep and so appalling, that since she could not speak of it without her blood freezing with dread.

From this abyss came frightful cries and unbearable exhalations; then she was seized with extreme horror;

---

[18] Editions Pierre Téqui, Paris, France, 1996.

but she heard the voice of her invisible conductor, who told her to have good courage, because no harm would happen to her. A little reassured by this friendly voice, she observed this door more attentively and saw that already very wide at its entrance, it was widening still more in its thickness; but in this dreadful corridor reigned unimaginable darkness; however a light was made for her, and she saw that hell was composed of three regions: one superior, the other inferior and the other intermediate.

Finally, in the upper region, everything announced serious torments; in the middle one, the torture device was even more frightening; But, in the most basic region, the suffering was incomprehensible.

Incredible for some but evident for the Christian believers! It is fairly safe to say, as described in the Bible (Ap 21,8 : *the fearful, and unbelieving, and the abominable, and murderers, and whore- mongers, and sorcerers, and idolaters, and all liars, they shall have their portion in the pool burning with fire and brimstone, which is the second death*), are already there, rest assured!

On this subject, we should now read the Lutheran thoughts on *The state of dead persons between death and resurrection*[19], although it is nothing new here.

---

[19] *Small lutherian dogmatic (Petite Dogmatique Luthérienne),* Tome 9, Dr Wilbert Kreiss, Centre de Documentation chrétienne, Sherbrooke, Québec, Canada, 2009, p. 251.

This is a question which has given rise to many divergent and contradictory doctrines, from the negation of the immortality of the soul to the theory of the sleep of the soul, passing by the affirmation of the possibility of 'a conversion after death, not to mention the purgatory and the limbo of Catholic dogma. It is said that the Old and New Testaments speak of a "stay in the dead" where the deceased wait for God in his judgment to rule on their fate. In the meantime, they are dead and experience neither joy nor suffering. It is true that the Bible speaks of a "scheol" in Hebrew and a "Hades" in Greek which is the place where all men go, good and bad (Genesis 37:35; 44:29; Job 10 : 21.22; 26: 5.6; Psalm 88: 4; 89:49, etc.).

Sometimes the term simply designates the grave (Job 14:13; 17: 13.14; Psalm 141: 7; Isaiah 38:18; Ezekiel 31: 15.16). But at other times it also denotes a place where the impious are punished: "The fire of my anger is kindled and it will burn to the bottom of hell" (Deuteronomy 32:22).

For the sage, the path of life leads upwards, so that he turns away from the grave (Proverbs 15:24) (...) Likewise in the New Testament, Jesus declares that Capernaum will be lowered because of his unrepentance "until hell" (Matthew 11:23), that the gates of hell will not prevail against his Church (Matthew 16:18, text where the term should clearly be translated as "hell", a word that Louis Segond's Bible does not know. The wicked rich man "was in torment" and suffered cruelly in hell, which is none other than hell (Luke 16: 22.23)., "dead" and "stay of the dead" are clearly distinguished from one another (Revelation 1: 8; 6: 8).

* * *

Heaven

After these two places, "purgatory" and "hell", let us now take a look at Heaven, before moving on to the Resurrection!

As one might expect, it is Christ again, who is best informed to speak about it. Dictated to the Italian mystic Maria Valtorta – already quoted earlier – in January 1944[20]:

See, Maria, how God loves all of you, how He loves you. No man, by any means, can reach the star nearest to the earth, the humblest one in its burning. But God grants that you–because He loves you and you love Him–may reach it, know it, and immerse yourself in its Fire. And consider that there is less distance between the earth and the stars than between the stars and the throne of God. They are the immense floor of the Heavenly City, more than the floor, they are its foundations. High up, much higher up, at inconceivable heights, for they do not correspond to human measures, is that blessed Reign ruled over by the Trinity, where a place is prepared for those who love. (...).

---

[20] The Notebooks 1944, Maria Valtorta, CEV, Isola del Liri, Italy, p. 312 and next.

Gilles Charles Vuille

First of all, then, last night I saw a sort of immense rose. I say "rose" to provide an idea of these circles of jubilant light which centred increasingly around a point of unbearable splendour.

A boundless rose! Its light was that which it received from the Holy Spirit. The most radiant light of eternal Love. Topaz and liquid gold turned to flame... Oh, I do not know how to explain it!

He shone forth on high, on high and alone, set in the immaculate and most radiant sapphire of the Empyrean, and from Him the Light descended in unending waves. This Light penetrated the rose of the blessed and of the angelic choirs rendering it luminous with its light, which is nothing but the product of the light of the Love that penetrates it (...).

And I saw God the Father. Radiance in the radiance of Paradise: lines of most radiant light, extremely white, incandescent. (...) Oh, how one sees that it is spirit! It is All. So perfect that it is All. It is nothing because not even the touch of any other spirit in Paradise could touch God. A most perfect Spirit, even in his immateriality. Light, Light, nothing but Light (...).

In front of God the Father was God the Son. Clothed in his glorified Body, upon which there shone the royal robe that covered his most holy Members without concealing his absolute and indescribable beauty. Majesty and Goodness fused into this Beauty. The scars of his five Wounds shot forth five swords of light over *all of Paradise and increased its splendour and that of his glorified Person. His smile was light, and his gaze light, light shone forth from his wondrous Brow, without wounds. (...) Jesus stood, holding his royal banner (...).*

I see that the Father, creates souls out of love for the Son, to whom He wants to give an ever-greater number of followers. Oh, how beautiful! They emerge from the Father like sparks, like petals of light, like globe-shaped gems in a way that I am unable to describe. (...) Beautiful, joyful to enter a body out of obedience to their Author. How lovely they are when they emerge from God. I cannot see, while I am in Paradise, when original sin sullies them.

(...) The Father acts from Love. The Son judges out of Love. Mary lives by Love. The angels sing out of Love. The Light exists because it is Love. Song exists because it is Love. Life exists because it is Love. Oh, Love, Love, Love! I annihilate myself in You. I rise again in You. I die as a human creature because You consume me (...).

[Christ]But since God's loving haste knows no delay, He, ahead of time, draws you into Himself in spirit and gives Himself to you with His Fire.

For the beauty of it, let us now read about the visions Saint Faustina Kowalska (1905-1938) experienced. As she narrated in her diary, on November 28, 1936, she was taken to paradise in ecstasy:

Today, I was in Heaven, in spirit, and I saw its inconceivable beauties and the happiness that awaits us after our death. I saw how all creatures give ceaseless praise and glory to God. I saw how great is happiness in God, which spreads to all creatures, making them happy, and then all the glory and praise which springs from this happiness returns to its source, and they enter into the depths of God, contemplating the inner life of God, the Father, the Son and the Holy Spirit whom they will never comprehend or fathom. This source of happiness is unchanging in its essence, but it is always new, gushing forth happiness for all creatures. Now, I understand Saint Paul who said: "Eye has not seen, nor has ear heard, nor has it entered into the heart of man what God has prepared for those who love Him". And God has given me to understand that there is but one thing that is of infinite value to His eyes, and that is love of God; love, love and once again love, and nothing can compare with a single act of pure love of God. Oh, with what inconceivable favours God gifts a soul that loves Him sincerely! Oh, how happy is the soul who already here on earth enjoys His special favors! And of such are little and humble souls. The sight of this great majesty of God, which I came to understand more profoundly and which is worshiped by the heavenly spirit according to their degree of grace and the hierarchies into which they are divided, did not cause my soul to be stricken with terror or fear; no, no, not at all ! (...).

*

As everything is possible for God, it seems obvious – excluding a few mystical people – that anybody can have access and see the Heaven, even alive, and then talk about it, upon return to earth. Now for many decades people of all races, confessions (or without!) and places, can be subject to an out of body experience, (the famous NDE – near death experience). One of the most spectacular known today is the one that abbot Jean Derobert, spiritual Padre Pio's son, experienced in 1958, as recorded in his book, only published in 2010: *Padre Pio, le transparent de Dieu*, Ed. Hovine, Lourdes, 2010. We should note that abbot Jean Derobert received a letter from Padre Pio one morning of August 1958 bearing two handwritten lines:

Life is a constant struggle but it leads to the light (underlined two or three times).

So here is part of this Testimonia:

That very night, a commando for the Algerian National Liberation Front attacked the village, killing everyone around, including myself. I "immediately had the experience of disembodiment," observing mine own body next to those of bloodied, fallen comrades, and then beginning a "curious ascension through a kind of tunnel."

In that "tunnel" were somber faces that emerged from a fog, "faces of people who did not have such a good reputation," had I to notice. As I went up, faces became more luminous. I was astonished to find that I could now walk and also see all around myself without moving my head.

I was also amazed that when my thoughts turned to my parents, who still living, were back in France, I suddenly found myself in the room they inhabited at my home, my parents asleep as I noted a piece of furniture that had been moved, describing it later to my mother, who asked how I could have known that. More fascinating still: when I thought of then-Pope Pius XII, I found myself in the Holy Father's room. "We spoke through the exchange of thoughts, since he was very spiritually attuned," which fact I had to testified of my alleged encounter with the sleeping Pontiff, apparently via a dream. The higher I went into the hereafter, the more beautiful and luminous it was,, until I found myself wrapped, in a paradise of soft blue light with thousands of other souls, then ascending still further, until I lost all human nature and became a "drop of light."

I have seen many other "drops of light," recognizing one as Saint Peter and another as the apostle John or Paul. I can testify that I next saw the Blessed Mother "in full radiance and beauty," smiling ineffably with Jesus—"looking spectacularly beautiful"—behind her. There I felt a total fulfillment of everything I could have ever desired. I also experienced perfect happiness.

When soon, I returned to the physical world—my face in the dirt, the bloody men around me once more—I found my own clothing pierced by bullets and full of blood. And still later, when I left the army, I went to see Padre

Pio at Saint Francis Hall at San Giovanni Rotundo. He motioned for me to come over and offered me a small sign of affection. Padre Pio then told me these simple words: "Oh! You really took me for a ride this time! But what you saw, it was really beautiful, wasn't it?" Halting, Padre Pio said nothing more. One understands now why I am not afraid any more of the death... as I know now what exists on the "other side."

Father Jean Derobert

*   *   *

Resurrection

Now let us move on to the next subject, an interesting one: the Resurrection! Historicaly speaking, it is worth refering to the Christian creed, mentioned on the first page, which speaks of resurrection and life everlasting, namely:

I believe in God the Father Almighty, Creator of Heaven and earth; I believe in Jesus Christ, His only Son, our Lord, He was conceived by the power of the Holy Spirit and born of the Virgin Mary. He suffered under Pontius Pilate, was crucified, died, and was buried. He descended to the dead. On the third day He rose again. He ascended into Heaven and is seated at the right hand of the Father. He will come again to judge the living and the dead. I believe in the Holy Spirit, the Holy Catholic Church, the communion of Saints, the forgiveness of sins, the resurrection of the body, and the life everlasting. Amen.

Previously, prophets of the Old Testament had already spoken of similar words.

Let us start with Isaiah, one of the greatest prophets of his time.

Here is his prayer[21] containing his cry.

Lord, in trouble have they visited thee, they poured out a prayer when thy chastening was upon them. Like as a woman with child, that draweth near the time of her delivery, is in pain, and crieth out in her pangs; so have we been in thy sight.

O Lord! We have been with child, we have been in pain, we have as it were brought forth wind; we have not wrought any deliverance in the earth; neither have the inhabitants of the world fallen. Thy dead men shall live; together with my dead body shall they arise. Awake and sing, ye that dwell in dust: for thy dew is as the dew of herbs, and the earth shall cast out the dead.

Witness of the Siege of Jerusalem (587 B.C.), the prophet Ezekiel is also the man who had a vision of the "dry bones" which will come to life again... a phase of the resurrection, namely[22] :

The hand of the Lord was upon me, and he brought me out in the Spirit of the Lord and set me down in the middle of the valley; it was full of bones. And he led me around among them, and behold, there were very many on the surface of the valley, and behold, they were very dry. And he said to me, "Son of man, can these bones live?" And I answered, "O Lord God, you know." Then he said to me, "Prophesy over these bones, and say to them,

---

[21] [1] Isa 26, 16-19.

[22] Ez 37, 1-6.

O dry bones, hear the word of the Lord. Thus says the Lord God to these bones: Behold, I will cause breath to enter you, and you shall live. And I will lay sinews upon you, and will cause flesh to come upon you, and cover you with skin, and put breath in you, and you shall live, and you shall know that I am the Lord."

And then men and nations form a unity. Furthermore, around 425 BC, the priest and scribe Ezra received, once again, revelations not only on the prophesy of Judgment day, hell, and heaven, but also on the Resurrection. Let us see that[23]:

And the Most High shall be revealed upon the seat of judgment, and compassion shall pass away, and patience shall be withdrawn; but only judgment shall remain, truth shall stand, and faithfulness shall grow strong. And recompense shall follow, and the reward shall be manifested; righteous deeds shall awake, and unrighteous deeds shall not sleep. Then the pit of torment shall appear, and opposite it shall be the place of rest; and the furnace of hell shall be disclosed, and opposite it the paradise of delight. Then the Most High will say to the nations that have been raised from the dead, 'Look now, and understand whom you have denied, whom you have not served, whose commandments you have despised! Look on this side and on that; here are delight

---

[23] IV Esd 7, 33 -37, Ecrits intertestamentaires (Intertestamental Scriptures), Editions Gallimard, La Pléiade, Paris, France, 1997, p. 1421.

and rest, and there are fire and torments!' Thus he will speak to them on the day of judgment.

This, in 400 BC, is simply incredible, exceptional! Later on, in 160 BC, it is Daniel — the man in the lion's den — who came to announce the resurrection of the deads. Here are his words[24].

And at that time shall Michael stand up, the great prince which standeth for the children of thy people: and there shall be a time of trouble, such as never was since there was a nation even to that same time: and at that time thy people shall be delivered, every one that shall be found written in the book. And at that time Michael will take up his place, the great angel, who is the supporter of the children of your people: and there will be a time of trouble, such as there never was from the time there was a nation even till that same time: and at that time your people will be kept safe, everyone who is recorded in the book. And many of them that sleep in the dust of the earth shall awake, some to everlasting life, and some to shame and everlasting contempt. And a number of those who are sleeping in the dust of the earth will come out of their sleep, some to eternal life and some to eternal shame.

Here again, this is astonishing. Simply remarkable! Just as remarkable as this statement on resurrection also

---

[24] Dn 12, 1-2.

found in the Old Testament. This is the surprising story of the martyrdom of seven brothers[25].

With his last breath, he said, Fiend though you are, you are setting us free from this present life, and, since we die for his laws, the King of the universe will raise us up to a life everlastingly made new.

If the Pharisees believed in resurrection, this was not the case for the Sadducees, to whom Jesus made the following retort[26]:

Are you not in error because you do not know the Scriptures or the power of God? (...) He is not the God of the dead, but of the living. You are badly mistaken!

It is worth noting that Jesus Himself announced His resurrection three times (Matt. 16:21, 17:22, 20:18–19), as well as His death[27]:

See, we are going up to Jerusalem. And the Son of Man will be delivered over to the chief priests and scribes, and they will condemn him to death and deliver him over to the Gentiles to be mocked and flogged and crucified, and he will be raised on the third day.

---

[25] 2 M 7,9.
[26] Mc 12, 24.27.
[27] Mt 20,18.

In the parable of the Good Shepherd, Jesus said the following[28]:

(...) And I lay down my life for the sheep (...) The reason my Father loves me is that I lay down my life only to take it up again. No one takes it from me, but I lay it down of my own accord. I have authority to lay it down and authority to take it up again. Tis command I received from my Father.

To express all the hope there is in the resurrection, St Paul also left us these words. Here is the first statement to the Galatians[29]:

I, Paul, an apostle—sent not from men nor by a man, but by Jesus Christ and God the Father, who raised him from the dead— and all the brothers and sisters with me, to the churches in Galatia. Grace and peace to you from God our Father and the Lord Jesus Christ, who gave himself for our sins to rescue us from the present evil age, according to the will of our God and Father, to whom be glory for ever and ever. Amen.

Here is the second one to the Thessalonians[30].

According to the Lord's word, we tell you that we who are still alive, who are left until the coming of the Lord, will certainly not precede those who have fallen asleep.

---

[28] Jn 10,17.

[29] Ga 1, 1-5.

[30] 1 Th 4, 15-17.

For the Lord himself will come down from heaven, with a loud command, with the voice of the archangel and with the trumpet call of God, and the dead in Christ will rise first. After that, we who are still alive and are left will be caught up together with them in the clouds to meet the Lord in the air. And so we will be with the Lord forever.

Further to this event, be also advised that some exegetes, historians - after in-depth investigations in recent times - concluded that 2030 could be the date of the famous Parousy, the Coming of the Lord, Jesus-Christ in His Glory.

As the first Passover[31] took place in 1.491 BC (Abib, then Nisan, according to the Hebrew calendar, now March-April in the current calendar, these latter months could complete the final date ... *as no one knows the hour and day* (Matt 24:36). Before then, the Tribulations (Matt. 24) will take place, and are envisaged to last 7 years, meaning that 2023 (March, latest September) signaled the beginning of said Tribulations.

To complete the picture, the prophet Daniel – already mentioned – has reported several days, weeks and months, namely 42 months and 1.290 days or 3 ½ years, in both cases (Dan 7 :25 and 12 :11- 12). The Book of Revelation also refers to these numbers, especially chap. 13 :5, 11 :2-3. Big sufferings of all kinds are to come.

---

[31] Robert Y. Jackson, *Jesus when is He coming ?* (AuthorHouse, Bloomington, In, USA, 2011), p. 15.

However, after the first 3 ½ years, further to the 3 days of Darkness, and the Enlightenment of consciences (see page 10), the Church (and her children, all believers in God, regardless their religion) will be caught, as said (1 Th 4 :16-17).

The non-believers, all those having denied God will then experiment their god, Lucifer, in charge of the whole world for the remaining 3 ½ years, completing the 7 years' Tribulations.

*   *   *

Immortality

As already stated, Immortality – originally – belongs firstly to the soul[32]. However, once resurected, the human body and its components will be identical to the glorious Body of Christ. As a matter of fact, the human body will become a glorious body, just as Moses saw (in Yahweh's times), or in Jesus times when Peter, John and James climbed Mount Sinai for praying, witnessing Him suddenly *transfigurated*, and discussing with Moses and Elijah (Luke 9, 28-36). Salomon gave us the following thoughts on the subject:

Because God did not make death, nor does he rejoice in the destruction of the living. For he fashioned all things that they might have being, and the creatures of the world are wholesome; There is not a destructive drug among them nor any domain of Hades [hell] on earth, (Wisdom 1,13-15).

Francine Bériault, a French-Canadian woman – previously quoted – also called "The Girl of My Will in Jesus", received in 2004 several messages from Christ

---

[32] Qo 12, 7. ... *And the dust returns to the earth as it once was, and the life breath [soul] returns to God who gave it.*

Himself regarding immortality. A word of warning: the tone is very different. It is as follows[33]:

Immortality is offered to you !

Life begins when God places his Life in the being that is forming in his mother's womb. My Life of a man was formed in Mary's womb to open the way to all those who were to enter into my glorious Being. No child who is impure after the Great Purification will be in my glorious Being, there will be only the elect of God the Father, for my Father has prepared everything so that his Son may be glorified in all things.

I am the Mystical Body of the Church, you are part of my Body. At this moment, I carry within me all the children of the world, not a single one is outside me since I allowed myself to be crucified out of love for all the children of the world. My love is so infinite! I knew there would be children who would not regret their sins, I still made my offering to the Father and my Father accepted my offering; he made my offering glorious because the Son is God. My Body of a man was glorified by my Father at the moment of the resurrection.

Today, I tell you that you will be glorified by the Son. My resurrection was a glorious moment that will never end, it reveals the love of the Father for the Son. And you who do not stop yourselves, or very little, to think that

---

[33] *Love For All My Children*, Jesus, Vol. 4, Editions Saint-Raphaël, Sherbrooke, Canada, 2004, § 313, p. 184.

I was carrying you, you do not grasp the greatness of the resurrection. Stop and try to understand what God wants to make known to you: "You who will pronounce your yes, your human life will be glorified by God. This will have an incredible impact on humans: you are mortal, you will be immortal. Your body and your soul will be united in order to be immortal."

My children, wake up from your torpor, it is high time that you become aware of my loving gesture. My resurrection is the gesture through which you will become immortal. Whoever wants to live in an immortal body must live my resurrection. To live my resurrection, you must want it. There is nothing that I, the Son of God, cannot accomplish, all was given to me by my Father. In a movement of love, I will take all of you within me and nothing that is of yourselves will be in motion, only I, I will do everything. You will all have to overcome the hurdle which is the presence of my Divinity, this will be done through the power of my Being; you will be pierced by a light and your being will be in my power, your soul and your body will reunite through my Divinity. My children, not one of you can grasp what will happen. (...).

Who among you would not be happy to learn that he will live eternally without knowing the death of the body? I, The Love, the Son of God, I tell you that you are the ones chosen to live on earth as immortal beings. (...).

I will show you your life within you; you will see everything about your life. You will know who your Father is, you will see his face, for whoever sees the

Son sees the Father, and you will not be able to deny your place in his plan of love. You cannot imagine the greatness of what Heaven reserves for you. You are the chosen of God, but also the only ones who will live this event in your flesh, therein lies the cost. You will have to prove your love to God. God wants you, he has prepared everything, but how many among you are ready? Many are not ready and the number is enormous.. ...).

Astonishing, what can we say after these revelations? In actual fact, a text, a path has been mentioned (but not to this extent) within the Book of Revelation, John 20:4-6 namely :

Then I saw thrones, where they took their seats, and on them was conferred the power to give judgement. I saw the souls of all who had been beheaded for having witnessed for Jesus and for having preached God's word, and those who refused to worship the beast or his statue and would not accept the brandmark on their foreheads or hands; they came to life, and reigned with Christ for a thousand years. The rest of the dead did not come to life until the thousand years were over; this is the first resurrection. Blessed and holy are those who share in the first resurrection; the second death has no power over them but they will be priests of God and of Christ and reign with him for a thousand years.

A side note to demonstrate that the Church, its officials, whose exegetes only attribute a spiritual value to this extract from the Scriptures (especially the thousand years part), and not symbolic, with the usual precautions – of course – while others think that it is the expression of a Jewish concept, of a messianic golden age, (Crampon's Bible). Finally, others might believe on the contrary that this Kingdom of a thousand years would signify that the coming of Christ allows already a genuine access to the heavenly life (TOB[34]).

To conclude, if the essence of the matter lies in hope – a Christian one initially – to arrive safe and sound, let us read Socrates' view, who set the benchmark with his wisdom, as mentioned in Georges Haldas' book *Socrates and the Christ*:

(...) Himself, in fact, declares it bluntly: the search for the truth has for its end - this is his own expression - "the improvement of our soul". And why that ? Because if death is, according to him, a change of residence, and that, in the latter one will be "in the company of the Gods" [Socrates, 400 years BC], we must, to be worthy of this company, to present ourselves with a soul liberated from terrestrial servitudes - and turpitudes – therefore, purified by the search, precisely for the truth. Inseparable therefore from our final destination (...).

With all the orders and prohibitions established, and the promised immortality waiting for us, it is therefore forbidden to be afraid of death ... while complying with a few rules, of course!

---

[34] *Traduction Œcuménique de la Bible (Oeucumenic Translation of the Bible), Editions du Cerf, Paris, France, 1998, p. 3058.*